Watercolour

and sketching for beginners

Watercolour

and sketching for beginners

p

This is a Parragon Book
This edition published in 2005

Parragon
Queen Street House
4 Queen Street
Bath BA1 1HE, UK

This edition designed by Design Principals
Cover by Talking Design

Drawings by Terry Longhurst
Text by Angela Gair and Theodora Philcox
Edited by Susie Johns and Theodora Philcox

ISBN-1-40545-610-8

Printed in China

Contents

Introduction

Drawing and painting are two of the first skills we develop as children. Through them we communicate, express our feelings, and often just simply enjoy the wonder of colour. Although one of our earliest skills, and despite the fact that the world we inhabit is overwhelmingly full of visual imagery, our culture gives priority to the spoken and written word. Before we know it, we lose the freedom with which we drew as a child and we can become embarrassed at our apparent incompetence.

Many of us just give up, only later to wish that we could do it! The good news is that we can. Given time and practice, everyone can draw, and this book is intended to show you how.

You don't need a vast array of expensive equipment to get started. Art shops contain a huge range of materials to seduce you, but a few pencils, a small selection of paints, including the three primary colours, and a couple of brushes will be enough to get you going. You can always add to these later as you gain more experience.

Once you have grasped the fundamentals, you will have the confidence to allow your natural creativity to take over and you can begin to forge your own path, bend the rules a little and discover your own unique way of representing the world.

In this book you will find an introduction to the materials and the effects which can be achieved using them. You will also find explained, simply and clearly, some of the underlying principles of drawing: tone and colour, composition, perspective and so on. These are all 'learnable' principles which, once mastered, will enable you to tackle any subject with confidence and enthusiasm. I hope the book will help you to discover your hidden artistic talents and inspire you to draw, draw, draw.

Getting Started

The pencil is the most familiar, natural drawing instrument. It is also the most versatile, capable of producing an infinite range of lines and marks. Pencil drawings can be done using lines alone, or by using tone alone without lines, or any number of techniques in between. The quality of a pencil line can be varied by the grade of pencil chosen, its sharpness, the way it is held, the degree of pressure applied, and the texture of the paper surface. Drawing pencils come in several grades, 'H' denoting hard and 'B' denoting soft. The HB (medium grade) is a good all-rounder, while an 8B (very soft) will give you a wide range of linear and tonal effects. Hard leads are suitable for precise lines and details, but in general they are less versatile than the soft leads.

Watercolours can be bought in pans (small slabs of solid paint), or tubes either singly or in pre-selected sets. You can also buy watercolours in two grades – artists' and student quality. Artists' quality paints contain higher concentrations of quality pigment, and will provide stronger, more luminous and transparent colour than student quality paints. Many artists advise you start with the best quality paints you can afford to give you the best chance of success, but you might feel inhibited using expensive pigments during your early experiments. Try both, and compare for yourself.

Different types of paper will give you different results. You can use any type of paper for sketching, but there are special papers for watercolour that give excellent results. You can choose from cold-pressed paper (also referred to as 'Not', because it is not hot-pressed!), which has a semi-rough surface, takes a smooth wash well, and is also good for detail, or Rough paper which has a more defined surface, or 'tooth', to hold the paint. This paper creates a more textured result as paint either settles in the hollows, or skates over the top, leaving flecks of white. Of the two, cold-pressed paper is the most versatile and easier for the beginner to handle. The third type, hot-pressed paper has a hard smooth surface which means paint tends to slide off it. It is great for detailed work, but not a good choice for fluid painting. Paper comes in various weights. To prevent buckling when using water, a paper of more than 140lb/300gsm should be used.

Pencils can make a wide range of marks from single lines to tonal areas created by blending soft pencil with a finger or cloth. Experiment using different grades of pencil and using them on their sides to make broad strokes, or their points to create textural marks. Cross-hatching can be sparse or dense to create varied areas of shadow.

Washes and Techniques

Colour washes form the basis of watercolour painting. They are thin layers of paint heavily diluted to maximise transparency. The following three pages describe and show a range of washes and painting techniques that, once you have practised and mastered them, will become the methods most used to produce your pictures.

It is important to keep the colours bright and fresh: you need to use plenty of clean water and rinse your brushes thoroughly after each colour application. Try not to 'muddy' the image with too many colours and keep reworking to a minimum to maintain the delicacy of the washes. Take the time to plan the sequence of washes you are going to use and apply them quickly and decisively.

Flat Wash

A flat wash uses one colour evenly across the paper. It can be achieved by wetting the paper, and then drawing a brush loaded with dilute paint across the area in a single stroke. This is then repeated again and again down the paper, with each stroke slightly overlapping the one above to pick up and blend with the wet edge.

Graded washes are achieved in the same way as a flat wash except that each stroke is more diluted than the last.

Graded Wash

Variegated washes use two or more colours. Once the first part of the wash has been applied using one of the colours, the brush is washed and then applies the next colour, partly overlapping the original colour, and blending wet in wet. Wet in wet painting is one of the key techniques of watercolour. Diluted paint can be applied either to damp paper, or added to another area of paint that is still wet. The colours will run into each other forming soft blends.

Variegated Wash

Wet on dry

Painting wet on dry allows for sharp edges in a painting. If thin washes of colour are painted over one that is dry, interesting transparent blends are achieved, resulting in stronger yet luminous colour. This technique is known as glazing.

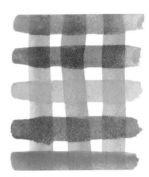

Glazing

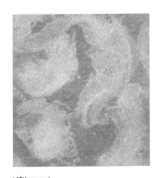

Salt

If rock salt is scattered over a wet area of paint the crystals will absorb the paint. Once the paint is absolutely dry the crystals can be brushed off leaving a variety of patterns depending on the grade of salt.

Salt

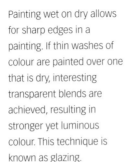

Lifting out

Paint can be applied with a sponge either to create washes or to produce textured areas depending on how dilute the paint is. Dry or damp sponges can also be used for lifting colour out. Colour can be lifted out to create soft highlights or clouds. Kitchen paper can also be used for this.

Sponging

Scratching out/Scraffito

Scraffito means 'scratched off'. When the paint is dry or nearly dry it is possible to drag a sharp implement such as your fingernail, a blade, or even the end of a brush through the surface, lifting the paint off in sharp lines.

If you draw a candle across your paper and then paint over it, the wax will resist the paint, leaving an interesting broken texture suitable for walls or rocks.

Wax resist

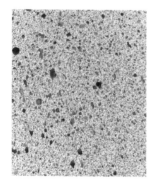

Spattering

Interesting textures can be achieved by spattering paint with a toothbrush or even using a spray device. Dip the toothbrush into the paint and then either draw your thumb or a piece of card swiftly across the bristles, and the paint will flick in small droplets onto your painting. Mask off any areas you don't want affected.

Fine Spattering

Colour

Colour can be used not only to describe objects, but also to suggest mood and atmosphere. The colour wheel will help you to understand how colour works and enable you to use it expressively in your paintings. The core colours are the three primaries – red, yellow, and blue – so called because they cannot be mixed from other colours. These are linked by the secondary colours, which are each mixed from two primaries: red and yellow make orange, yellow and blue make green, red and blue make violet.

Colours that are next to each other on the wheel are described as harmonious because they share a common base colour. Harmonious colours create a unified image with no jarring notes. Pairs of colours that are opposite each other on the wheel are known as complementary pairs. When placed side by side they intensify each other, thus a patch of red looks more vibrant when juxtaposed with green.

One half of the wheel comprises warm colours – reds, oranges, and yellows – and the other comprises cool blues, greens, and violets. Because warm colours appear to advance and cool colours to recede, the use of warm hues in the foreground and cool ones in the background accentuates the illusion of depth and atmosphere in landscape paintings.

The colour wheel is a simplified version of the colours of the spectrum, formed into a circle. It is a handy reference for understanding the way colours relate to each other. The arrangement of colours on the wheel shows the relationship between the primary colours and their opposite, or complementary colours, and their adjacent colours.

Colours that lie opposite each other on the colour wheel are called complementary colours. When a colour and its complementary are placed next to each other they intensify each other; when mixed together they neutralise each other.

Drawing Simple Shapes/Rendering Form

The most basic forms to be found in nature – the cube, the sphere, the cone, and the cylinder – can be used to simplify your understanding of any object you paint, no matter how complex.

When you come to paint complicated subjects – the human figure, buildings and trees in landscape, fruits and flowers in a still life – it helps to visualise them first as simple geometric shapes. All the objects around us are combinations of the curves and planes found in the sphere, the cone, the cylinder, and the cube. A building is basically a cube; most fruits and vegetables are roughly spherical; a bottle and a tree trunk are basically cylinders; poplar trees are conical in shape, as are some flower heads. Learning to see objects in terms of simple shapes that can then be broken down into smaller, more complex shapes, helps us to paint them more easily and accurately.

The difference between flat, two-dimensional shapes and solid, three-dimensional forms is the way light falls on objects, creating shadows, half-tones and highlights that reveal their planes and surfaces. In painting, this is represented using tone and shading – in other words, degrees of light and dark.

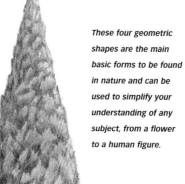

Any shape in nature, from a flower right up to a mountain, can be worked out in simple three-dimensional terms. It was the great artist Cézanne who said, "Treat nature in terms of the cylinder, the sphere, the cone…"

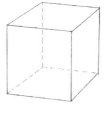

These four geometric shapes are the main basic forms to be found in nature and can be used to simplify your understanding of any subject, from a flower to a human figure.

Practise modelling form by drawing outlines of the four basic shapes and then converting them into objects by filling in the outlines with tone.

Apply charcoal to the darkest part of the sphere and blend it with your finger to show how it curves towards the light.

On rounded objects the tone changes are gradual, following the curve of the surface as it turns away from the light. The highlight is at the point nearest to the light source.

An eraser can be used to pull out highlights and reflected light.

On rounded forms, the shadow side may lighten slightly near the outer edge. This is caused by light being reflected back onto the object by nearby surfaces.

Tone can be built up in line. Using a pencil or pen and ink, try hatching and cross-hatching, increasing the density where the shadows are deepest.

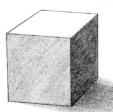

Where edges are sharp, as in the cube, there are clearly defined planes of light and shadow.

Cast shadows vary in size, tone and shape according to the angle and distance of the light source.

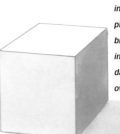

Use a pen to draw a cube and then fill in the shadow planes with a brush and diluted ink. Build up the darkest tone with overlaid washes.

Contour Shapes

An outline is a flat shape that describes only two dimensions. A contour drawing describes all three dimensions – length, width, and depth – because it follows the bumps and hollows within the form.

Drawing most often involves using line to describe the three-dimensional quality of an object. The line must describe the bulk of the form and not just its outline. If you draw the outline of a figure, for example, it looks flat, like a cartoon character. There is no information in the drawing to tell us that the arms, legs, and so on are actually rounded. But as soon as you work across the drawing with a few simple contour lines that describe the bumps and hollows created by the bones and muscles, the way the hair lies, and the creases in the clothing, the figure becomes solid and three-dimensional – even without shading.

A contour drawing is rather like a contour map: it travels across the forms, indicating where the surface of the object is close to us or further away, where it is curved and where it is flat. By making subtle changes in the width and weight of the lines you can also describe the fullness and 'weight' of the forms.

The best way to describe objects accurately and make them look convincingly three-dimensional is to draw them as though they are transparent. By drawing both what is seen and what is hidden, you don't just describe the outer shape of an object, you get a better sense of its underlying structure and this helps you to draw it more accurately. You can rub out any unwanted lines later if you want to, though they often add 'texture' to a drawing.

This outline drawing conveys very little information about the three-dimensional qualities of the forms, so they look flat.

Here, contour lines are introduced which map out the curvature of the apples, explaining their forms.

This method is especially useful when drawing cylindrical objects like cups, bowls and vases. If you draw the entire base of the object, and not just the bit you can see at the front, it will appear solid and planted squarely on the surface. You will find it much easier to draw the elliptical shape of the opening accurately, too.

If you drape a piece of striped fabric and then draw it by copying the stripes, you will see how the stripes become contour lines that describe the three-dimensional curves and folds in the fabric.

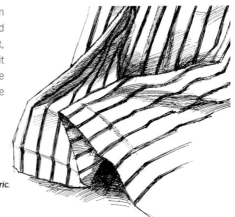

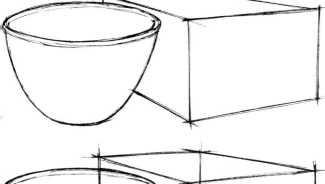

This bowl and box, drawn in outline only, look a bit lopsided and one-dimensional.

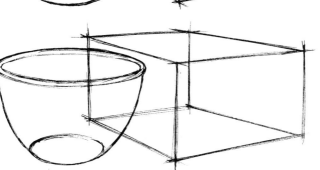

Imagine that the objects are transparent and draw them that way. The shapes are now more accurate and appear solid and real.

Simple Perspective

Perspective is a system used by artists to create a convincing illusion of three-dimensional form and space on a flat piece of paper. The basic principles are very straightforward.

Before you can paint anything in perspective, you must first establish the horizon line. If you can't see the actual horizon (in a town, for instance), just remember that the horizon is at your own eye level. The horizon level will change according to whether you are sitting down or standing up but it is always directly in front of your eye.

Vanishing points

The basic assumption of perspective is that parallel horizontal lines that recede into the distance appear to converge at a single point on the horizon, at the centre of vision. This is called the vanishing point. All lines above your eye level will slant down to the vanishing point and lines below your eye level will slant up to the vanishing point.

One and two-point perspective

One-point perspective refers to a situation where there is only one vanishing point at the centre line of vision. However, objects are often viewed from an oblique angle. If you are drawing the corner of

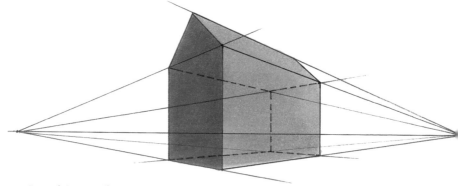

Two-point perspective

Each side of this house is seen at an angle of roughly 45 degrees to the picture plane. Each side appears to recede towards a vanishing point on the horizon line on the left and right of the image. To draw the building, start with the nearest vertical line and assess the angles at which the sides of the building recede from it. Extend these lines to the vanishing points. Using this framework you can now draw the windows and doors in perspective.

a building, for instance, you would need to plot two vanishing points, at which the converging lines of each side of the building meet.

With two-point perspective it is likely that at least one vanishing point, and sometimes both, will be outside the picture area. You have to imagine the vanishing points in the space beyond your page and estimate the angles of the building by eye.

1 *To draw a row of arches or windows in perspective, showing how they appear narrower as they recede, first plot the horizon line and the lines of the top and bottom of the building converging towards the vanishing point.*

2 *Draw a line from halfway up the first upright to the vanishing point. Draw in the second upright. Take a diagonal line from the top of the first upright through the centre of the second. Where it meets the base line, position the third upright. Repeat until you reach the end of the building.*

When drawing figures which are receding into the distance, plot converging lines from the nearest figure to the vanishing point. You can then draw the distant figures to the correct size in relation to the foreground figure.

Aerial Perspective and Viewpoint

Aerial perspective is a further development of linear perspective. This term describes a natural optical illusion caused by the presence of water vapour and dust particles in the atmosphere. These affect visibility, making colours, tone and forms appear less distinct the further away they are. The most effective means of creating the illusion of depth in your paintings, particularly in landscapes, is by using tone and colour to recreate the effects of aerial perspective.

Imagine that you are standing in a field with the landscape stretching away as far as the eye can see. As your eye travels from the foreground to the horizon you will notice that colours which appear warm and bright close up gradually become cooler, paler, and bluer as they recede towards the horizon. Tones and tonal contrast appear strongest in the foreground and become progressively weaker in the distance. Texture and detail also become less distinct the further away they are. To create the illusion of deep space in your landscape paintings, all you have to do is to mimic these effects, making your tones and colour fade gradually towards the horizon.

Placing the horizon

Take time to observe your subject from different viewpoints and to make several sketches of it. You will be surprised how even small changes of viewpoint can dramatically alter the perspective and the impression of depth in the scene. The sketches here demonstrate how altering the horizon can create a very different sense of space, and add drama if positioned either very high or very low.

A useful tip for representing the effects of aerial perspective in monochrome is to visualise the landscape almost as a series of vertical, receding planes. The foreground plane is strongest in tone and detail; the middle ground and background planes become progressively paler and less distinct as they get closer to the horizon.

In landscapes, placing the horizon in the centre of the paper has the effect of dividing the composition in two, leaving the eye undecided where to go. It is best to place it a little above or below centre so that you can emphasise either the foreground or the sky.

An imaginative viewpoint can make for a more striking image. Looking at the landscape from a high viewpoint is fascinating because it is relatively unfamiliar. Why not climb up to the top of a hill and sketch the scene rolled out before you.

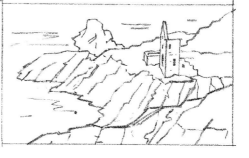

Looking at a scene from a low viewpoint also offers a fresh perspective on the landscape. If you position yourself at the bottom of a slope, for instance, a building at the top of the slope will tower dramatically above the horizon line.

Composition

When you begin a painting, the first thing to consider is the composition. Good composition means arranging the elements in your subject to create an appealing and well-balanced drawing that attracts and holds the viewer's attention.

It is important that the centre of interest is positioned with care. Never place it in the middle of the picture as this produces a static arrangement; position it off-centre so as to create a visual tension that gives a more lively effect. The rule of thirds is a good guideline to follow. Also, avoid having two objects of equal interest in a drawing as they will vie for attention; if a scene contains two trees, for example, make one bigger than the other, of a different tone, or push one further back.

The secondary elements in the painting should be arranged so as to take the eye on a gentle journey from foreground to background, or from one object to another. Look for lines or implied lines that follow through the picture and link one area to another, such as a meandering road or river curving up through the scene, or the contours of cloud formations, or even shadows cast on the ground.

The composition should appear balanced and harmonious, while containing enough variety to entertain the eye. For example, the rounded forms of fruits, flowers, jugs and bowls in a still life repeat and echo each other, creating a satisfying harmony; at the same time, visual interest is achieved through varying their shapes, sizes, colours, and tones.

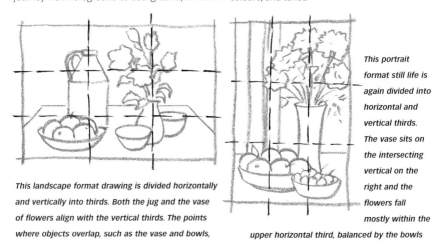

This landscape format drawing is divided horizontally and vertically into thirds. Both the jug and the vase of flowers align with the vertical thirds. The points where objects overlap, such as the vase and bowls, are positioned close to where lines intersect.

This portrait format still life is again divided into horizontal and vertical thirds. The vase sits on the intersecting vertical on the right and the flowers fall mostly within the upper horizontal third, balanced by the bowls of fruit in the lower third.

The sketches shown opposite demonstrate traditional methods of dividing up the picture area to achieve a balanced design. The 'rule of thirds' is a simple mathematical formula based on the principles of harmony and proportion. Imagine the picture area divided into thirds, horizontally and vertically; any strong horizontal or vertical elements in the sketches should coincide with these lines, and the points where two lines intersect are good places to locate the focal point of the drawing.

This Japanese bonsai tree creates a pleasing curvilinear composition. The outline of the tree fits loosely within a circle and the eye naturally follows the twists and curves of the branches up, around and down.

Arrangements based on an underlying geometric shape break up the picture in a pleasing way. Here, a still life is loosely grouped within the shape of an equilateral triangle. This construction has a natural stability, enhanced by grouping the objects so that they overlap each other.

Make sure that your focus of interest is placed off-centre. Here the curved path draws the eye to the focal point, which is located at the intersection of thirds.

Using a Viewfinder

It can sometimes be difficult to decide what to draw when confronted with a landscape. Start by taking a walk round with your sketchbook and a cardboard viewfinder and note down anything that grabs your attention. From any one position there may be several directions of view that offer subjects to draw. A viewfinder will help you isolate a particular section of a subject.

With practice, a viewfinder will help to train your eye to see potential subjects and to compose them well. When the scene is concentrated within the window of the frame, you can see at a glance how it will look on paper. Bring the viewfinder closer to your eye to include a wide-angle view; hold it away from you to select a small area. Raise or lower it to alter the position of the horizon line, depending on whether you want to emphasise the sky or the landscape features. Don't forget the rule of thirds, many landscape paintings are divided into one-third sky, two-thirds land (or vice versa); no one quite knows why, but the human eye finds that this proportion has a pleasing balance. And remember too, don't just look at your subject horizontally; you can turn the viewfinder upright and work with it in a vertical format to good effect.

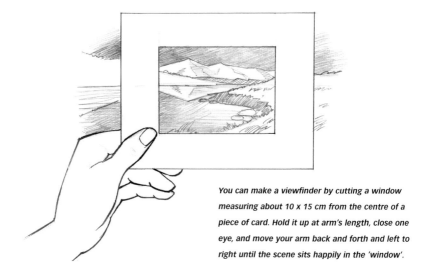

You can make a viewfinder by cutting a window measuring about 10 x 15 cm from the centre of a piece of card. Hold it up at arm's length, close one eye, and move your arm back and forth and left to right until the scene sits happily in the 'window'.

With the horizontal (landscape) format
the eye can roam from side to side and
the mood is one of calm and restfulness.

With the upright (portrait)
format the vertical elements
become more dominant. The
mood becomes more
enclosed and intimate.

This sketch conveys a strong sense of space
on a small scale by means of both the sharp
perspective of the centrally placed road and
the set-back position of the focal point.

Composing a Landscape

No matter how breathtaking a landscape view is, you may find that you have to select and rearrange the elements of the scene in order to create a more balanced image.

Once you have chosen a landscape view, walk around it with your viewfinder and make rapid sketches to see how the composition looks on paper. Try to forget, for the moment, about 'trees, fields and clouds' and think instead of 'lines, shapes and tones'. These elements should be arranged on the paper so that there is one main area of interest, supported by secondary features which lead the eye from the foreground, into and around the picture, eventually coming to rest at the focal point.

Start by breaking the scene down into large, simple areas based on sky, horizon and foreground. Make sure the horizon doesn't cut across the middle of the paper as this creates identical spaces on either side of it, which is boring. Position it in either the upper third of the picture or the lower, depending on whether you want to emphasise the sky or the land. Place the focal point somewhere off-centre, at a point that is a different distance from each edge of the paper, thus creating balance.

Try to ensure that similar shapes are echoed throughout the picture, knitting the diverse elements together. At the same time, introduce subtle contrasts that entertain the eye: angular and flowing shapes, busy areas and quiet areas, light and dark tones, bright and muted colours.

Close-up

Mid-distance

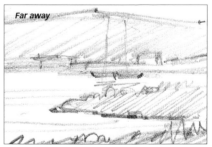

Far away

These three sketches show how even a slight change of viewpoint can alter the balance of shapes and tones, and even the mood, of the scene. A soft pencil is ideal for making thumbnail sketches because you can get down the features and the tonal areas quickly.

For a simple landscape, an uneven division of land and sky is usually preferable to a mid-page horizon. By making the foreground the largest area, you can add to the illusion of space and depth. Opt for a low horizon if you want to emphasise a dramatic skyline.

Natural features of the landscape often provide strong cues for the arrangement of a composition. In this sketch, the curve of the country lane sweeps down from the foreground, leading the eye into the middle distance, where it is then led upward in a criss-cross fashion by the linear patterns of fields and hedgerows to the distant hills.

Pencil Landscape

The ordinary graphite pencil has a freshness and immediacy that makes it ideal for outdoor sketching. It is very versatile, capable of suggesting light and atmosphere, space, and depth.

Make sure you choose the right grade of pencil for your sketches. An H pencil will only give a pale line, no matter how hard you press, whereas a soft pencil such as a 6B can be controlled by pressure to give lines of varying weight and thickness, as well as a wide range of tones from light to dark. Soft pencils are ideal for drawing landscapes on location. They are speedy and easy to work with, helping you to capture a scene quickly and with minimum fuss – essential when you are working outdoors in changeable conditions.

If you have access to the countryside, why not find a scene that appeals to you and spend a few hours drawing it with just a couple of pencils – say, a 2B and an 8B. A view like this one, with hills, fields, and woodland stretching to the horizon, presents a particular challenge; without the benefit of colour, you have to rely on lines and tones alone to create a sense of spatial recession.

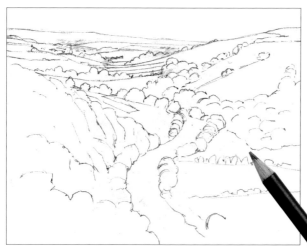

1 *Using a 2B pencil, start by plotting the position of the horizon line. Then lightly sketch in the curve of the river, which establishes the perspective of the scene. Briefly outline the important contours of the hills, fields, and trees, remembering to make them smaller as the scene recedes towards the horizon. The whole effect should remain free and sketchy at this stage.*

2 *You can now start to build up tone and detail. Use the softer 8B pencil to work gently over the darker parts of the scene with hatched lines. Vary the pressure on the pencil to create a variety of tones, and alter the direction of the strokes to capture the natural features. Don't work up any one area at a time – build up the drawing as a whole, moving freely all over the paper to ensure a harmonic result.*

3 *Continue to develop the various tones and texture in the scene: use long, evenly spaced hatching for the smooth fields and short lines and scribbles for the trees. Suggest spatial recession using a progression from strong to light tones and a diminishing scale of textural marks into the distance.*

Watercolour Landscape

It is more often than not the landscape that inspires a novice to pick up the brush, and it is with landscape that watercolour comes into its own. Fluid, transparent, fresh and fast, it is the ideal medium to capture the passing moods of nature, ever-changing with the light. Ideally, landscapes should be painted on location rather than from photographs: a picture painted directly from nature has a freshness and an immediacy that cannot be reproduced in the studio.

Although watercolour is a spontaneous medium, you have to work methodically in order to keep your work fresh and lively; too much fiddling will result in muddy, overworked washes. Take the time to plan the sequence of washes you are going to use and apply them quickly and decisively. Always work from light to dark: start by laying pale tones in thin, broad washes and work up to the dark tones with successive applications of thin layers of colour. Establish the large colour masses first, working broadly with the largest brush you can. Leave the detailed refinements till last, added with a smaller brush if necessary.

Working with a limited range of colour is not only practical for outdoor work – the less equipment you have to carry the better – it is also better for your painting as you will be more likely to achieve a harmonious colour balance. A variety of landscape greens, for instance, can be created mixing together just one yellow and one blue; by using more blue in the mix you make darker, cooler greens, and by using more yellow you make lighter, warmer greens. And because the same colours are repeated throughout, it helps to tie the image together and give it a satisfying unity.

1 *Tape a piece of Not surface watercolour paper to a board, or use a sketching block, and sketch out the composition very lightly with an HB pencil. It's best not to draw the outlines of the clouds as you want them to be soft, loose shapes. Then dampen the paper with clean water.*

2 *Use a limited palette containing French ultramarine, lemon yellow, and raw sienna and a medium size round brush. Start by painting in the sky leaving ragged shapes for the clouds. Paint the undersides of the clouds using raw sienna. Note the perspective of the clouds, which appear darker, smaller and closer together as they near the horizon. Then block in the cornfield, trees and haystacks, mixing the ultramarine with the lemon yellow for the greens, and the raw sienna for the cornfield.*

3 *Let the painting dry and then apply layers of stronger colour, gradually building up the forms with thin overlays. Use darker tones of green to model the forms of the trees and haystacks with shadow. Use the tip of the brush to add the finer details.*

Sketchbook Studies

Sketching regularly will increase your manual dexterity and your powers of observation. It is only by looking and by becoming familiar with the small details of the subject that you can achieve the confidence that enables you to create drawings and paintings with real conviction.

It is a good idea to buy a small sketchbook that can fit into your pocket or bag so that you can always carry it around with you. All good artists keep copious notes and sketches as reference material for their work, and you should use your own sketchbook to build up a personal record of visual ideas and information.

Trees make a fascinating study in themselves. Draw them all year round and observe their shapes and growth patterns, from the skeletal winter outline to the abundant masses of summer foliage. In landscapes, trees are usually seen from a distance, so it is more important to capture their overall shape than to try to draw every leaf and twig. In fact, too much detail can render a tree lifeless. Sketch in a rough outline to get the overall shape, and then look for the broad shapes made by clumps of foliage.

Several quick sketches, even unfinished ones, can be as valuable as a single, involved study. They solidify your understanding of the overall structure and shapes of your chosen subject.

The transparency of watercolour is ideally suited to sketching soft clouds and misty skies. Individual cloud studies can be beautiful things in their own right and will provide you with invaluable reference for painting.

Evergreen trees such as alders and cedars tend to be angular in outline, with dense masses of dark foliage.

Here a quick pencil sketch has been enhanced with simple watercolour washes to create a lively impression of an oak tree in all its summer glory. Notice that the foliage is not a solid mass; there are lots of 'sky holes', particularly around the outer edges of the tree. Paint the sunlit foliage first, with light, warm greens. Whilst the paint is still just damp, apply successive layers of cool, dark bluish greens for the foliage in shadow.

Sketching with Paints

Watercolour paints are ideal for colour sketching outdoors because they dry quickly and the few materials and tools required to use them are easily packed into a small shoulder bag.

Fluid washes of watercolour paint can be used to introduce colour and tone to line work in pencil, coloured pencil or pen and ink. They are especially effective for on-the-spot sketches of the landscape: fast and fluid, they capture the freshness and spontaneity of the subject.

What you will need

Watercolour equipment is tailor-made for sketching outdoors – light and easy to carry. A box of dry pan paints will be lighter than tubes and the inside of the lid provides a mixing palette. A single brush is all you need: a good quality brush will hold plenty of paint for washes and come to a fine point for details. If you are using a sketchbook, make sure the paper is thick enough to take a wash: anything less than 300gsm (140lb) will buckle when wet washes are applied.

A very quick study using pen and waterproof ink overlaid with watercolour washes. Accents of white paper convey the effect of bright sunlight, which produces strong highlights on the water's surface and on the heads, shoulders and forearms of the figures.

This sensitive watercolour study was painted on a pre-stretched watercolour pad. Note how the dark, solid shapes of the groynes accentuate the luminosity of the sky and water.

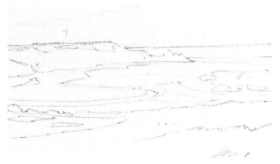

1 *All you need to paint this landscape sketch is a piece of watercolour paper with a slight 'tooth', a pencil, a sketcher's pocket box of watercolours, a medium-size round brush, a bottle of water and a water pot. Start by lightly sketching out the composition in pencil.*

2 *Using the traditional watercolour technique of working from light to dark, establish the basic forms and local colours with thin, broad washes. Keep your paints fluid and transparent: this allows light to reflect off the white paper, which is what gives a watercolour its characteristic luminosity.*

3 *Apply the mid-tones, then the darkest tones, waiting for each area to dry before you add another wash. Keeping additional painting to a minimum and leaving much of the base wash visible gives the finished sketch a pleasing harmony.*

Buildings – Choosing a Viewpoint

Whilst the countryside provides endless inspiration for atmospheric landscapes, towns and cities should not be overlooked for artistic potential. There are many aspects to explore in the urban environment, from closely observed details of individual buildings to entire streets bustling with people and cars.

This beautiful country house with a grand curved drive sweeping up to the front door cried out to have its 'portrait' painted.

No matter how grand and imposing a building might be, its construction is still basically that of a cube, or a series of cubes. If you can draw a box in perspective, you can draw a building in perspective, and once you've got that right, the rest – doors, windows, chimneys, and balconies – will just fall into place.

Choosing a viewpoint

When a house is the main focus of interest in a picture it's important to show it to advantage and bring out its individual character. Walk around the site and find the best, most flattering angle of view. Decide whether you want to move in close, or

include some of the surrounding scenery. The light is important, too, as shadows can help to explain forms and accentuate details and textures. As a rule it is best to avoid painting or drawing in the middle of the day, when the sun is high in the sky and casts minimal shadows. Most artists prefer early morning or late afternoon, when the sun casts long, descriptive shadows.

This house is viewed at a 45-degree angle, so two-point perspective comes into play. Two of its walls are visible, so there are two sets of perspective lines converging towards two vanishing points on the horizon line. As you can see from this picture, an oblique viewpoint enhances the scale and grandeur of the building and stresses its three-dimensional volume and solidity.

1 *Make a careful drawing of the house with a well-sharpened pencil. Start by lightly indicating the horizon line. Draw the vertical line at the front edge of the house. Draw the angles of the receding planes of the roof and extend these to the horizon line to fix the vanishing points on either side of the house. It is now a relatively simple task to complete the overall shape of the building and to establish the angles of the doors and windows. Then you can lightly indicate the landscape setting.*

2 *Paint the sky and trees in the background and leave to dry before painting the main colours of the house. Then put in the foreground grass and flowers and the foliage along the front of the house. Allow the painting to dry.*

3 *Suggest the window panes with tiny squares of medium and dark tone, leaving thin slivers of white paper for the glazing bars. Apply transparent dark washes over the shadow end of the house, under the eaves and beneath the windowsills. Suggest the pattern of the brickwork and add more detail to the foliage.*

Sketching Details

As well as complete buildings, it is rewarding to make sketches and studies on site of specific details, patterns and textures which you can use as a reference for a more considered painting back home.

Buildings are often rich with details that give them individual character and make them fascinating subjects to paint. With older buildings, in particular, features such as doors, windows, arches, balconies and architectural mouldings can make intriguing subjects in themselves. When you are walking around city streets, keep a sketchbook handy so you can jot down anything of interest. A simple pen or pencil will describe the delicate tracery of wrought iron gates and balconies with calligraphic lines; or you could use watercolour to record colourful verandas and shop awnings that create lively patterns within the overall framework of a shopping street.

When you paint a street scene, it isn't necessary to define every window, brick and roof tile – a small area of texture can imply the whole. Broken brush strokes, dots and dashes will give an impression of intricate detail while gentle washes convey volume and solidity, and the play of light and shadow. With experience you will develop a kind of visual shorthand that suggests rather than labours over the details of buildings.

Don't be too precise when drawing windows. Here, the edges of the colour washes don't follow the lines of the glazing bars exactly, and most of the glass panes are left unpainted, helping to integrate the window into its surroundings.

Careful study of the shadows creates solidity and monumentality in this small pencil sketch of an old stone doorway. Notice the gradation of the shadow inside the arch. Hold the pencil on its side for broad shading and use the point for picking out linear details.

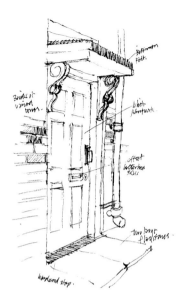

Pen and ink is a medium which is very effective in recording buildings and architectural details. As well as an overall sketch of the subject, you can make written notes about colours, tones and intricate details.

Many subjects suitable for detailed pencil work can be found on buildings. Here a 3B pencil records the intricate arrangements of bricks and tiles on the corner of a house.

When a building is viewed from ground level, vertical perspective comes into play. Use your pencil to check the angles of the receding lines of roofs and chimney stacks.

Still Life – Setting Up

A still life is one of the most straightforward subjects for the beginner. You can choose what objects make up the arrangement; to a large extent you are in control of the lighting; you won't get wet or frozen; and your subject won't move!

Setting up

When setting up a still life, don't be tempted to include too much. A few simple objects, selected for their qualities of shape, form and texture, will give you plenty to explore and enjoy.

Generally, still lifes work best when they have a kind of theme; one that has caught your attention and perhaps has a naturally harmonious composition or colour. For example, you might choose objects which are related through association – flowers and fruits, kitchenware and foodstuffs, plants and gardening implements being the most obvious examples. Or you might be drawn to particular objects for their pictorial qualities – shape, colour, tone, texture, pattern – and the contrasts and affinities they display when grouped together.

Consider the overall shape of the group you have arranged on the table. Look at it through a viewfinder and decide whether it fits more comfortably within a horizontal or an upright format. Here, for example, a fairly high viewpoint emphasises the vertical forces within the group and so an upright format is appropriate. The same group drawn in a horizontal format would be surrounded by too much empty space.

Composing the group

When you have arranged your still life, move around it and sketch it from different angles and viewpoints to see which makes the better composition. Each change of angle and viewpoint presents fresh possibilities, and you can extend those possibilities even further by using a viewfinder to home in on small sections of the group to create exciting 'cropped' compositions.

There is plenty to think about: does the light cast descriptive shadows that emphasise the form of the objects? Is there a reasonable variety of shapes and tonal contrasts? Examine the relationship not only between the objects themselves but the spaces between them as well; these 'negative' shapes should balance and enhance the 'positive' shapes of the objects, creating a cohesive design.

This group obviously fits more comfortably into a horizontal format. Try to arrange your still life in a way that emphasises the form and structure of the objects and the spaces between them. Study how each object relates to the others and be aware of spatial relationships. Small adjustments – moving an apple in front of a vase instead of next to it – will give a sense of depth to the drawing.

Textures and Details

The ability to convey texture is vital if you want your drawings to look realistic. Texture provides an opportunity to create decorative interest in a drawing that enlivens the overall composition.

When suggesting a particular texture, consider the full range of marks available to you: short, choppy strokes; nervous, wavy lines; small stippled dots; long curves and loops; even blurs, smears and spots. You can also create an illusion of texture by mirroring the tonal patterns that textures create and by bringing out the ways in which different surfaces reflect light.

Capture the hard, knobbly surface of a pineapple with heavy outlines, applying more pressure in the shadow areas. Hatch in each segment, modelling the tiny raised ridges with light and shade.

Glass reflects a lot of light, so use mostly pale tones and leave white paper for the sharp, bright highlights. Keep your shading as even as possible to convey the smooth glassy surface.

The graceful curve of a bird's feather is one of nature's marvels. Here the silvery tones and delicate marks made by a well-sharpened 2B pencil capture form and texture with a sensitive touch. Try drawing feathers with a fine-nibbed dip pen and sepia ink, too.

This coffee mill makes an attractive subject on which to practise drawing cubes and ellipses. The half-opened drawer adds interest to the drawing by breaking up the outline of the square base.

Crumpled paper forms stiff folds and distinct planes – qualities which you can bring out with hard contour lines and finely hatched shading in the shadow areas, leaving white paper for the sharp highlights.

Textures and Details

As you experiment you will see that some media and surfaces have inbuilt textural qualities that can be adapted to suit a particular subject. Charcoal dragged on its side across a coarse-grained paper will, for example, produce broken, textured marks that might suggest a rugged cliff face or a gnarled tree trunk. Ink wash on smooth paper lends itself naturally to conveying smooth glass and metal surfaces. Equally, though, you can render an animal's soft fur in pen and ink, or draw a delicate flower with charcoal – it's all in the handling.

Gather leaves from different tree species and record their different shapes and contours – smooth, toothed or lobed – in a sketchbook. Try to express the different textures of the leaves you have collected using hatching, cross-hatching and broad sweeps laid in with the side of the pencil.

Try using mixed media to capture the distinctive characteristics of flowers. Here, for example, the lily petals were washed in freely with watercolour and allowed to dry. The delicate striped markings were then picked out using coloured pencils.

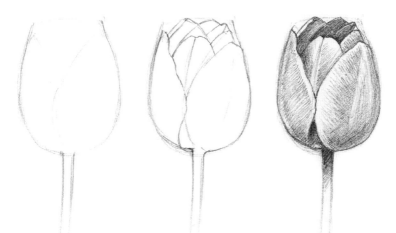

Start off by drawing flowers with simple, well-defined shapes, such as tulips. Using a 2B pencil, draw the outline shape with delicate, sketchy lines. Draw the inner petals, varying the strength of your pencil lines to convey the delicacy of the petals. Finally, make diagonal hatching lines to show the light and shade created both by the way the light falls on the flower and by the form of the flower itself.

The transparency of watercolour is ideal for the fragile forms of flower petals. Note where the lightest lights are and leave these as white paper. Before applying the first delicate wash, gently dampen the area to be painted with a fine brush. Apply increasingly darker tones to the flower while the underlying washes are still damp so that they merge to form subtle, translucent effects; if the paper is dry, the washes will dry leaving a noticeable line.

People – Proportion and Measurement

Of all the subjects that an artist is likely to tackle, the human figure is undoubtedly the most challenging. If you can learn to draw and paint faces and figures well, then you will be able to draw anything competently. Learning to interpret accurately the proportions of the body and at the same time instil a feeling of life into a figure, is a real test of the artist's skills. Constant measurement and re-assessment while you work will help to ensure that your painting is an accurate rendition of your subject.

With a few simple rules as a guide, you will find that drawing the human figure is much less difficult than you might have thought. Figure drawing requires a higher degree of accuracy than most subjects. It doesn't really matter if the tree in your landscape drawing is slightly misshapen, but in a figure drawing, if the head is too small or the legs too short, it will be very noticeable.

Proportions of the figure

It is helpful to know the proportions of the 'ideal' figure so that you can use them as a guide to accuracy when drawing people. Most artists use the head as a convenient unit of measurement. In a standing figure, the height of the head fits into the rest of the body approximately seven times. The mid-point is not the waist, as is commonly assumed, but just above the crotch. With the arms by the side, the hands reach halfway down the thighs. The feet are generally about one head length long – a common mistake is to draw them too small. These are useful guidelines but don't use them as a substitute for direct observation; few of us have perfectly proportioned bodies!

The proportions of the body change as we grow and develop. The average adult body is approximately seven heads tall; a young child's body is about five heads tall and an older child's about six heads tall. These proportions provide a useful starting point but you will find that individual sitters often vary slightly from this average.

Measuring

Use a pencil and your thumb to check the proportions of the figure as well as angles such as the slope of the shoulders or hips. Hold your pencil vertically, extend your arm fully, close one eye and look at the model. Align the top of the pencil with the top of the model's head and slide your thumb down until it aligns with the chin. Keeping your thumb in place and your arm fully extended, move the pencil to the measurement you want to check. Always hold the pencil at arm's length, with your elbow locked; if you bend your arm your measurements will be inaccurate.

When the weight is on one leg, the angle of the shoulders runs contrary to the angle of the hips so that the body balances itself. Drawing an imaginary vertical down the centre of the body will help you to work out the variations in symmetry between the two sides of the figure.

Foreshortening is what happens when one part of a form is nearer to you than another. Here, the model's thighs are going away from the viewer and so appear shorter than they are in reality. If you look at the figure as a two-dimensional shape, you will find it easier to draw the foreshortened outline convincingly. Learn to trust what your eyes tell you! Use your pencil and thumb as a measuring tool to check key angles and proportions on the body.

Drawing the Head

When drawing portraits you will find it easier to achieve an accurate likeness if you have an understanding of the physical structure of the head and the proportions of the face.

Before tackling an actual portrait drawing, practise rendering some simple head shapes and learning how to position the features correctly in relation to the head. The basic form of the head is determined by the bony structure of the skull. This can be visualised as an upside-down egg shape with the wider end representing the top of the head. Having established the shape of the head, you can position the features, and here the 'rule of halves' is a useful guide. First, draw a vertical line down the centre of the head to mark the position of the nose and the centre of the lips. Then draw a horizontal line across the centre of the head: this marks the position of the eyes and from here it is easy to gauge the eyebrow line. Sketch a line midway between the eyebrow line and the top of the chin in order to find the position of the base of the nose. Then draw a line midway between the base of the nose and the tip of the chin to find the line of the lower lip.

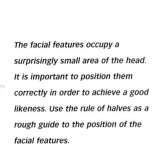

The facial features occupy a surprisingly small area of the head. It is important to position them correctly in order to achieve a good likeness. Use the rule of halves as a rough guide to the position of the facial features.

Now you can sketch the features. The gap between the eyes is approximately the width of an eye. The ears line up between the eyebrows and the tip of the nose. The hairline normally sits about one-third of the way down from the crown of the head.

Do bear in mind that the rule of halves is intended only as a guide to the 'average' face. Each individual is different and it is the variation from the norm that gives a face its distinctive character. Check proportions and relationships by measuring with your pencil.

When the head is tilted upward, downward, or to one side, the features appear foreshortened. As with the foreshortened figure, it can be difficult to accept these distortions until you learn to look at them logically.

When the head is lowered, the cranium appears larger and the shape of the face contracts. The steeper the angle of the head, the less of the face is visible. The features appear compressed. The tip of the nose may overlap the mouth and the ears are positioned higher than the eyes.

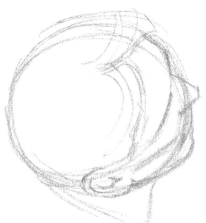

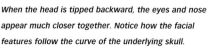

When the head is tipped backward, the eyes and nose appear much closer together. Notice how the facial features follow the curve of the underlying skull.

Informal Portraits

To develop your skills in figure and portrait work, why not start by making informal studies of your family and friends? Informal portraits are the artistic equivalent of a snapshot, in which the subject is dressed casually and adopts a relaxed and natural pose. They can be great fun to do, and the result, if successful, is a lively image that captures the personality of the sitter more readily than a formal portrait might.

If possible, persuade a friend or family member to pose for you for a couple of hours at least. This will give you plenty of time to try out different poses and make preliminary sketches. When setting up your model you need to find a position that is comfortable for him or her, and one that creates an interesting shape. In this pose the model is sitting down with the legs drawn up and the arms in a comfortable position. This creates a relaxed, natural pose that is also visually pleasing: the varied angles of the legs and arms set up a series of rhythms that give life and animation to the drawing and lead the eye around the picture.

Foreshortening

Perspective makes things appear to shrink as they recede, so that if you look at a seated model from the front you will see that the thighs appear compressed in length. Foreshortened shapes can appear extreme and you many want to alter them to make them more recognisable. But you must force yourself to draw what you see, not what you know. To help you get the shapes and proportion right, use the pencil-and-thumb method described on page 47. You might also like to make a quick sketch before you begin your drawing.

1 *Sketch in the main outlines of the figure with a 6B pencil. Hold the pencil loosely, well back from the point, and make light, tentative marks – hard outlines make the figure look wooden. Avoid too much rubbing out; when mistakes occur, leave them in and draw the more accurate lines alongside. These re-stated lines give life to the drawing.*

Start by sketching in the overall outline of the figure with fluid lines, making sure that it will fit comfortably on the page. Draw with your whole arm, not just your fingers. Only when you have something resembling the pose should you return to specific areas and start to tighten them up.

2 *Once you are happy that the outline of the figure is accurate, rub out the guidelines and start to tidy up the drawing – though still avoiding making hard outlines. Indicate the positions of the facial details and the outline of the hair. Start to emphasise the important lines, making them heavier where they project forward and lighter where they recede.*

3 *Half close your eyes so that you can see the areas of light and shadow. Apply loose hatching to the shaded areas of the face and limbs. This will make the figure appear more solid and three-dimensional. Finally, apply more pressure with the pencil to add dark tones to the hair, sweater and shoes.*

Sketchbook Studies

It's a good idea to get into the habit of carrying a pocket sketchbook around with you, in order to make lots of rapid sketches of figures as often as you can.

Regular sketching is the best way to learn how to portray figures convincingly, so get out and about and sketch people in everyday situations as often as you can. Find a suitable location where people tend to congregate and linger, such as cafés and restaurants, train stations, museums, and art galleries. At the beach or in the local park, people walking dogs, playing games, or sitting on benches provide ample models. Stores and markets, sports arenas, and construction sites offer the challenge of sketching moving figures. The possibilities are endless.

Drawing in public places calls for courage and self-confidence, but with a pocket-sized sketchbook and a simple pen or pencil tucked in your pocket, a sketch can be made in a few minutes, even a few seconds, and it can be done discreetly. You don't have to think in terms of making a finished drawing: just jot down what you see at a glance. Keep things small and simple. Speed is of the essence, so try to grasp the essentials – the overall shape, posture, and action of the figure. Don't be discouraged if your first attempts are inaccurate or too tight – the more you do, the more intuitive your drawings will become.

Choose a spot where your subjects are unaware that they are being sketched, allowing you to catch lively expressions and movements.

31/5/96

blonde hair.

white blouse

very pale / subtle yellow/ green

black skirt Black Tights

black fittings

black shoes.

Bars are an excellent source for characters, expressive gestures and incidental details. This sketch was drawn with waterproof ink and watercolour wash.

grey sweatshirt pale Blue Jeans

black shoes.

Leopard skin

Bhn Black

A journey on public transport need not be boring if you carry your sketchbook with you. Trains, buses, and aeroplanes are great places for people-watching, and if you manage to draw discreetly and catch people unawares, you can produce marvellous character studies.

A quick, spontaneous sketch can often be more incisive and expressive than a highly finished drawing because it captures the essentials of character and gesture.

Sketching Children and Babies

Sketches and drawings are a wonderful way to capture those precious moments of childhood that are over all too soon. But you have to learn to be 'quick on the draw'!

Drawing young children is always a challenge because they never keep still for long. Start off gently by drawing a child asleep, or absorbed in a favourite book or TV programme. At least you will stand half a chance of getting something down on paper! When you feel brave enough, progress to sketching children on the move. The secret is speed and practice. If you have children at home, keep your drawing materials readily to hand and try to make at least one sketch of them every day. Your pace of drawing will increase and you will begin to develop methods of rapid notation that enable you to catch a fleeting pose or expression.

As children move about and play, make several sketches on a single sheet and dart from one to the other. Put down your impressions with simple, unfussy strokes and concentrate on the outline shapes and gestures of the figures – don't worry unduly about details such as faces and hands.

Selecting a medium

To capture the charm and innocence of children, and their energy and enthusiasm, you will need a medium that is both rapid and sensitive. Soft pencil is a good 'instant' medium that can also be smudged with a finger for soft tones. Very quick sketches can be made by smudging soft pastel or charcoal to catch the overall shape of the pose, then drawing in the details with the point of the stick. Gentle watercolour washes are perfect for delicate sketches of babies and young children. The contours of the face and body are much softer in children than in adults, so modelling should be kept broad and simple.

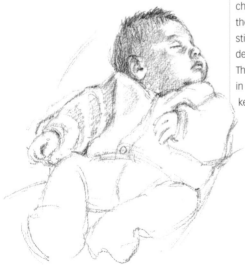

A baby has a very large head in comparison to its body. It has very rounded, large cheeks and the eyes, nose and mouth are crowded into a small area of the face.

A light, sensitive touch with a soft pencil conveys the soft, rounded cheeks and delicate features of these young girls. Try to match your drawing style to the nature of the subject: light, tentative strokes will convey childlike qualities better than hard, continuous outlines.

These simple pencil sketches capture the charm and innocence of young children at play. Making quick, sketchy drawings of moving children helps to develop your speed and confidence so that you are better able to capture something of the energy and vitality of your subjects.

A Portrait in Watercolour

Watercolour is an excellent medium for spontaneous, informal portrait studies. Its fluidity and translucency are perfectly matched to the subject, bringing out the delicate, living qualities of skin and hair.

The secret of sketching portraits in watercolour is to work systematically and confidently, keeping your washes as clear and fresh as possible. Inexperienced painters often make the mistake of using the paint too thickly and overworking the skin tones, with the result that the skin appears muddy and lifeless. The beauty of watercolour is that delicate, transparent washes allow light to reflect off the white paper beneath, creating an impression of the skin's natural luminosity.

In keeping with traditional watercolour practice, always start with very pale, diluted colours and gradually strengthen the tones with successive washes laid one over the other. It is important to keep the colours bright and fresh: you need to use plenty of clean water and rinse your brushes thoroughly after each colour application. Try not to 'muddy' the image with too many colours and keep reworking to a minimum to maintain the delicacy of the washes.

The skin appears lighter and warmer in the prominent light-struck areas, such as the cheeks and forehead, and darker and cooler in the shadow areas. Because warm colours appear to advance and cool colours to recede you can use these warm and cool contrasts to model the contours of the face and figure, much as a sculptor pushes and pulls a block of clay. In this portrait, for instance, notice the warm yellows on the cheek, the chin, and the bridge of the nose, and the subtle hints of cool blue in the shadows of the face and arm.

1 *Make a light pencil drawing of the model, carefully studying the relative proportions. In this pose the arm is nearer than the face and so appears large in comparison. When the drawing is complete, rub out any unwanted lines, leaving an image that is clear enough to guide the painting but doesn't interfere with the delicate washes of watercolour.*

2 *Dampen the figure with water and block in the palest flesh tones. Model the contours of the face, arm and hair with successive washes of darker, cooler colours. Keep the paint fluid and allow the colours to merge on the damp paper to suggest the softness of the flesh.*

3 *Apply your colours with confidence and do not attempt to tidy up the loose brush strokes too much – the portrait will look much more lively if you allow some of the brush marks and ragged edges to show rather than blending them neatly together.*

4 *Strengthen the colours over the whole image, developing the structure of the face and arm with a series of overlapping washes. Define the tresses of hair with curving brush strokes, letting the pale underwash show through to suggest highlights and individual wisps of hair. Define the eye and mouth with dark colour applied with the tip of the brush.*

Animals – Basic Shapes

Drawing and painting animals and birds presents a problem similar to that of drawing young children – they cannot be asked to pose for you, so you will have to rely on preliminary sketches, photographs, and a knowledge of the basic structure of the creature.

Start by drawing animals from photographs and progress to drawing your own pet if you have one. Look for the basic underlying shapes: from the side, a cat's head forms a roughly ovoid shape and the ears are small, elongated triangles. A dog's head fits into a square or hexagonal shape, depending on the breed, and the body is shaped like a kidney bean. All animals can be visualised as a series of simple, interlocking geometric shapes – circles, ovals, triangles, and rectangles. Once you are familiar with the basic shapes of animals, you will find it easier to sketch them from life, with fluid lines and rhythmic gestures that capture their grace and movement.

Simple outline drawings like these are fun to create. They show how it is possible to draw the basic body structure of any animal, large or small, by seeing it as a collection of interlocking geometric shapes. Side views are the simplest to start with.

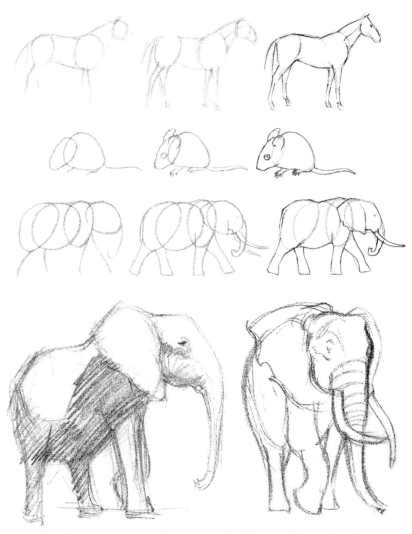

As you gain confidence, try drawing animals on the move. Watch them carefully to feel how their entire bodies move, and still working with your basic shapes, try to find the lines that sum up the movement.

Sketching Animals

Animals don't keep still for long, so quick sketches are important resources for larger paintings. Family pets make the best models since they are always around and you can make studies of them sleeping, eating or gazing out of the window.

Start by sketching your cat or dog sleeping. This gives you the chance to learn about structure and proportions, which will enable you to draw a moving animal quickly and accurately. Next, try sketching your pet while grooming, it will remain fairly stationary but perform a series of repeated movements, which will allow you to record the rhythmic grace of the pose. Have several sketches of different poses on the go at once, and dart around the page as your subject shifts position. This is quite a challenge but you should end up with a page of interesting studies.

Mice, hamsters, and gerbils are lively little animals. The speed and suddenness of their movements make them hard to draw – you just have to sketch rapidly as they skitter about. This sketch was done with an ink pen and then washed over with watercolour.

Proportions are important in capturing the individuality of your pet. The big ears, long tail, and gangly limbs tell us that this is a puppy.

The wiry, long-haired coat of this Border collie is depicted by making the pencil strokes follow the direction of the hairs.

Watercolour is a good medium for conveying the texture of fur if you simplify the furry texture into broad areas of tone rather than attempting to paint each hair. Apply quick, directional brush strokes over an almost-dry underwash to suggest the thick, rug-like fur on the dog's body.

Details and Textures

The textures, colours and patterns of fur, feathers and scales are a rewarding area of study when drawing animals. Try to find marks that will represent them with conviction, but without overstatement.

When you are drawing animals and birds you will find that their patterns and markings can help to describe the underlying form. The stripes of a tiger or a tabby cat, for instance, follow the contours of the body and give it a feeling of solidity. Your first priority, however, is to get down the structure and proportions of the body. Only when you have got the shape and pose right should you start to tackle details and patterns.

It is essential to find a quick, shorthand way of describing an animal's texture or coat pattern. If you try to draw every spot, stripe, hair, or feather your drawings will look lifeless and overworked. Observe where the most distinctive markings are and use them to emphasise the shape of the

animal in key places such as around the head, shoulders and rump. The eye fills in the gaps, so a few carefully placed marks are read as a complete pattern or group of hairs.

Be expressive with your mark-making to bring out the character of a texture. Short fur can be imitated with hatched lines; the tonal gradations across the body built up by varying the density and pressure of the marks. Draw animals with long, smooth hair using broad areas of tone with occasional lines to suggest the rhythms of its fall. Pay attention also to the shadows and highlights on the fur or feathers as they help to describe the structure of the body beneath.

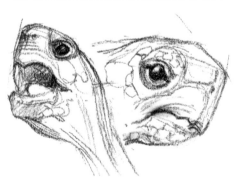

When drawing the scaly skin of reptiles, a feel for the rhythm of the markings will be more characteristic than the minute reproduction of every detail.

Coloured pencils were used here to portray the hamster's sleek, velvety, colourful fur with short, fine lines that follow the contours of the form. The tiny highlights on the eye are important in conveying their brightness.

It is possible to capture the formidable beauty of a large bird of prey in a zoo, where the confined situation encourages the birds to sit still for long periods of time. Watercolour is a suitable medium for recording detailed impressions, conveying the bird's bulk and the structure of feathers with delicacy and freedom.

The complex whorls and ridges on a tortoise's shell are a delight. However, you don't have to reproduce each individual scale. In this study, watercolour washes were used to suggest the patterns with a 'lost and found' quality that implies their continuation around the creature's form.

Index